latin dance

Isabel Thomas

Published in 2012 by Wayland

Wayland
Hachette Children's Books
338 Euston Road
London NW1 3BH

Wayland Australia
Level 17/207 Kent Street
Sydney NSW 2000

Concept by Joyce Bentley

Commissioned by Debbie Foy
and Rasha Elsaeed

Produced for Wayland by Calcium
Designer: Paul Myerscough
Editor: Sarah Eason

Photographer: Adam Lawrence

British Library Cataloguing in Publication Data

Thomas, Isabel, 1980–
    Latin.
    1. Ballroom dancing—Juvenile literature.
    2. Dance—Latin America—Juvenile literature.
    I. Title
    793.3'3-dc22

ISBN: 978 0 7502 7741 9

Printed in China

Wayland is a division of Hachette Children's Books, an Hachette UK company.

www.hachette.co.uk

Acknowledgements: Getty: Ian Gavan/ Stringer 8–9; Photolibrary: Age Fotostock 6 tr; Rex Features: SNAP 15; Shutterstock: Akva 14tr, Efanov Aleksey Anatolievich 1, 2cl, 6cl, Anky 16tr, Marcelo Roberto Caba cover, 3br, Dmitry Matrosov 23tr, My New Images 23tl, Damian Palus 22br, Jack Qi 26–27, Simone Simone 16bl, Stepanov 2–3, Aleksandar Todorovic 26cl, Valua Vitaly 23br, Gary Yim 2b, 4–5, 30, 30–31.

Note: To indicate the gender differences in the step by step spreads, M refers to a male dancer's steps and F to a female dancer's steps.

cover stories

the**people**

the**moves**

the**talk**

LATIN DANCE

Flamboyant and passionate, Latin dance is one of the most expressive and energetic dance forms. It has a rich and colourful history.

African influence

In the sixteenth century, many African slaves were brought to Latin American and European countries. They brought with them their own music and dance that featured new rhythms and beats. These rhythms soon spread to other Spanish-speaking countries and fused with native Latin dances found there. The result was a variety of dynamic and fast-paced dance styles such as the salsa, samba, cha cha cha, rumba and tango.

Exotic dances

Many governments and religions were against these new dance styles. For example, the sensuous samba, which was brought by African slaves into Brazil, was seen as a sinful dance by the Europeans.

Dance evolution

Over time, as dance has evolved, new styles have borrowed moves from Latin dances. Ceroc, for example, is a fusion of salsa, hip-hop, ballroom, tango and jive. Television has played a part, too. Dance programmes have helped to make Latin dance more popular than ever. Long live Latin!

Dance checklist

- Good rhythm and timing
- Strength and stamina – some dances are demanding
- A sensational hip wiggle!
- A sense of style and drama

Type 'Latin dance championships' into www.youtube.com to see what the passion and heat of Latin dancing is all about!

tango

salsa

rumba

paso doble

THE DANCES

Latin dances are famous for their fast rhythms and intricate footwork. Dancers do not just listen to the music, they feel the rhythms and tell a story with their moves.

Salsa!

This sizzling party dance is packed with fast, intricate turns and sassy hip movements. As dancers let their weight settle onto each leg, they push the hips out to the side. The upper body stays straight and level, for the ultimate hip wiggle!

Tango drama

Originating in Argentina, the tango is about the relationship between a man and a woman. It is famous for its slow, powerful steps, staccato movements, passionate holds and expressive, storytelling gestures.

Rumba love story

The passionate rumba is famous for its sensual hip action and quick spot turns. Dancers keep the waist loose, letting the hips sway from side to side. Intense eye contact turns the dance into a romantic love story.

Paso doble passion

Dramatic paso doble dancers step as though they are marching or stamping, holding the head and chest high. Sharp arm and hand movements tell a story of passion.

Cheeky cha cha cha

Super-fast synchronised moves are the main focus of the cha cha cha. Light footwork is a must to keep up with the bubbly rhythms. This dance has a distinctive 'step, step, cha, cha, cha' rhythm to follow.

cha cha cha

BRIAN FORTUNA

THE STATS
Name: Brian Fortuna
Born: 20 September 1982
Place of birth: Philadelphia, USA
Job: Professional dancer, choreographer and instructor

Brian burns the floor with Ali Bastian!

Early years

Brian has dancing in his genes. Both of his parents are successful Latin dancers who own a dance school. They began teaching him to dance when he was four years old. By his teens, he was so good that he was following in his parents' footsteps and teaching dance himself.

Following his dreams

Brian studied business at university, but decided to follow his passion for performing. He moved to Los Angeles and landed small TV presenting jobs on *Dancing with the Stars* and *American Idol*. At the same time, he taught dance and choreographed Latin dance teams.

On the big screen

Brian's reputation as a great dance teacher soon won him work in Hollywood. He choreographed and danced in the TV drama *South Beach*, and featured as a dancer in the film *The Aviator* (2004), which starred Leonardo DiCaprio.

Visit Brian Fortuna's website at www.brianfortuna.com to see videos and pictures of him in action.

Making it big

In 2007, Brian joined the hit US show *Dancing with the Stars* and was partnered with former Miss USA, Shandi Finnessey. The following year, he appeared in the UK version, *Strictly Come Dancing*, for the first time. In 2009, he partnered popular UK soap star Ali Bastian on *Strictly*. Brian's choreography and skills helped them to achieve the first-ever perfect score in the Viennese waltz!

Dance passion

Brian is passionate about getting people dancing. In 2010, he choreographed the TV show *Dancing on Wheels* – featuring wheelchair ballroom and Latin dance. In the same year, he turned up the heat on stage with Ali Bastian in the West End hit *Burn the Floor*. When it comes to Latin dance, Brian scores a perfect 10!

Career highlights

2003 won the North American Amateur Latin Championships

2004 starred in the Canadian documentary *Live to Dance*

2007 performed at the Oscars and won the Christmas special of *Strictly Come Dancing*

2010 released *Latin Jam*, a collection of music for street salsa – his favourite dance

2011 earned the What's On Stage Award nomination for Best Newcomer for his performance in *Burn the Floor*

LOVING LATIN!

Harriet Bell's story

I was 14 when I began ballroom and Latin dancing. One of my best friends had danced in a national competition and it sounded so glamorous. I'd done other styles of dancing, but just hearing about Latin made me want to do it! At my first dance class I fell totally in love with Latin's energy and rhythm.

I soon discovered that Latin dance is really social and I made a lot of new friends. Once we'd mastered the basics, a group of us entered our first competition. I was so proud when my partner and I got through to the final round and were placed second for our cha cha cha! The fun of competitions isn't just about you dancing; it's about watching other dancers' styles and picking up tips to improve your own.

After the competition, I stepped up my class and practice time to 15 hours a week, including helping out in the beginners' classes. My dancing improved quickly and I began to compete at national level. I love taking part in shows and contests – the whole floor suddenly comes alive and all you can see is a whirl of gorgeous, colourful dresses and people smiling and having fun!

These days dancing takes up lots of my time, but I will never for a moment regret starting Latin dance. I love to watch reality TV dance shows and dream that one day I will be as good as some of the professional dancers. I definitely think I'm at my happiest when I dance – I usually have an enormous grin on my face. Latin is so special and nothing can take that away from me.

H Bell

BASIC SALSA

Salsa is an energetic party dance that is lots of fun! The movement is mainly in the hips and legs, and this basic salsa move is a rocking step, forwards and backwards.

You will need:

- space to dance
- a dance partner
- salsa music

1

F Hold your partner's hands. Step backwards with your right foot and put your weight onto it.

M Hold your partner's hands. Step forwards with your left foot and put your weight onto it.

FEEL THE BEAT:
Salsa Dance Break by Destiny's Child

2

F Step forwards with your right foot, bend your left knee and lift your left foot off the floor.

M Step back with your left foot, bend your right leg. Lift your right foot off the floor.

Type 'salsa steps for beginners' into www.youtube.com to see the basic steps in action.

3

F Step forwards with your left foot and rock forwards on it.

M Step back with your right foot, rocking backwards on it.

4

F Bring your right leg forward to join your left leg. Bend your right knee. Start again with step 1.

M Bring your left leg back to join your right leg, bending your left knee. Start again with step 1.

Got it?

Fluid salsa moves involve transferring the weight from one leg to the other which, in turn, moves the hips. Watching people dance the steps (see YouTube link above) will help you get a feel for this.

COME DANCING!

From school gym lessons to prime time Saturday night TV, Latin dance fever is enjoying a popularity explosion! So how did sassy samba, salsa and tango moves become such a big hit?

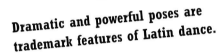

Dramatic and powerful poses are trademark features of Latin dance.

Seen it in the movies

The 'Latin boom' in America in the 1930s and 40s created a range of new musical styles. Hollywood films of the time helped to bring the style, poise and glamour of Latin dance to a worldwide audience – for example, *Rumba* (1935) showcased popular Latin dance styles. The 1980s saw a surge in Latin dance popularity, helping to make the 1987 film *Dirty Dancing* become a massive box office success and one of the best-loved movies of all time.

On the small screen

Successful Latin American singers such as Ricky Martin, Shakira and Enrique Iglesias all helped to bring Latin music and dance to a wider audience during the 1990s.

In the early 2000s, the trend for celebrity TV contests and reality shows led to a dance-based version, *Strictly Come Dancing*. It pairs professional dancers with celebrities in a ballroom and Latin dancing tournament. The show, together with the US version, *Dancing with the Stars*, has given Latin dance superstar status and encouraged increasing numbers of viewers to take it up for themselves. An amazing 30 countries around the world now have their own versions of the smash hit TV show.

The love story

The theatre has not escaped the Latin dance bug, either. Twenty years after the movie *Dirty Dancing* opened, the stage version became a worldwide hit, from London's West End to Broadway!

The Latin success story shows no sign of ending soon. From TV to theatre and dance classes, the public's love affair with Latin dance is still burning strong. These dances are sassy and hot – and they are heading to a ballroom near you

The slick Latin dance routines of *Dirty Dancing* turned its stars Jennifer Grey and Patrick Swayze into dance film legends.

LATIN LANGUAGE

Here's a quick and easy guide
to the Latin lingo in this book.

bateria
a percussion band that plays
samba music

batucada
a type of extremely
fast-moving samba

ceroc
a popular type of dance
that mixes Latin with hip-hop
and jive

choreographer
a dance teacher who puts
moves to music to create
dance routines

flamenco
a style of dancing that
originated in Spain. It is very
rhythmic and involves dramatic
hand claps and foot stamps

jive
a lively dance that originated
in the United States in the
1940s. It involves fast-paced
leg kicks, flicks and spins

matador
the Spanish word for
a bullfighter

passistas
the male dancers in the
Rio de Janeiro carnival

promenades
the powerful, striding steps
used when dancing the tango

sambadrome
the parade ground in which
samba is danced during the
Rio de Janeiro carnival

sashay
to shake the hips

shimmy
a dance move in which the
dancer shakes the hips
and shoulders

spot turn
a turn used to change direction
when dancing the rumba

surdo drum
a large drum played by a
samba drummer

Viennese waltz
a type of ballroom dance that
originated in Vienna, Austria

matador

GLOSSARY

adrenalin
a hormone found in the body that causes the heart to beat faster and gives the dancer a 'rushing' feeling

beading
tiny beads that are sewn into fabric to add decoration or detail to dance costumes

bodice
a piece of clothing that fits firmly around the chest and waist

float
a vehicle that is covered with decorations and driven through the streets as part of a carnival parade

fused
joined or combined

hip-hop
a style of music and dance that originated in the 1970s in the USA

intricate
very detailed and complex

perfectionist
a person who wants to meet the highest standards in anything they do

plumes
large, showy feathers often used on headdresses or costumes

sensuous
passionate and expressive

spangles
small sparkling objects (such as sequins) that are sewn onto costumes for decoration

staccato
in music, a word for short, separate notes

synchronise
when dancers coordinate their movements in time to music

SIMPLE TANGO

FEEL THE BEAT:
Toxic by Britney Spears

If you like drama, you will love the tango. This dance features close body contact, promenade steps and staccato head movements.

You will need:

• space to dance
• a dance partner
• tango music

1

F Turn your head to look away from your partner. Place your left hand on your partner's right shoulder.

M Hold your partner's right hand out to the side. Look towards your hands. Place your right hand on your partner's back.

2

F Step backwards onto your right foot.

M Step quickly forwards onto your left foot, keeping your right leg stretched behind you.

3

F Step backwards onto your left foot.

M Step forwards quickly onto your right foot.

4

F Step quickly backwards onto your right foot.

M Step forwards quickly onto your left foot.

5

F Mirror your partner's move with your right leg. Then flick your head forwards.

M Slide your right leg forwards to join your left leg. Slide your left leg out to the side.

Type 'tango steps for beginners' into www.youtube.com to see the basic steps in action.

Got it?

The tango is a dramatic 'striding' dance, which should be strong and proud to reflect the beat of the music. Steps 1 to 4 are a series of strong, driving steps in which the couple travels across the floor. Step 5 is a finishing flourish to the dance.

19

A WEEK IN THE LIFE OF LATIN DANCE COMPETITOR

MATT TWEEDALE

blog   **news**   **events**

Monday

It's the first day of my dancing week and I helped to teach the beginners' Latin and ballroom classes at uni. Teaching really helps me to perfect my own dance technique because I get to practise the simple steps that are a core part of our team's routines.

Tuesday

I worked on my fitness and stamina this morning, with an hour in the gym followed by an hour of swimming. Our dance class was amazing this evening! We developed a flashy new salsa routine, then finished the night with some jive dancing to Christina Aguilera's *Candy Man*. It was great fun and it helped us all relax.

Wednesday

No gym today – I wanted to give my body time to recover. Instead I had a leisurely breakfast – yoghurt, muesli and fruit – before my training session with the dance team to prepare for Saturday's national dance competition. My partner Ruth and I ran through our

blog   news   events

cha cha cha about ten times! After all that practice I know our footwork is going to be spot on!

Friday

I spent the morning packing for the competition. We take lots of luggage to competitions because we need our competition dress as well as everyday clothes. The girls have even more bags because of their hair styling gear, accessories and make-up! In the afternoon we set off for the hotel where we were staying for the event.

Saturday

Competition day! Around 900 couples were taking part in the whole event. The atmosphere was tense and everyone was so excited. The Latin section was in the afternoon. Ruth and I were couple number 137 and we were thrilled to get through to the quarter-finals with our cha cha cha and jive routines. This put us in the top 32 couples out of the 600 contestants taking part in the Latin section!

After the Latin section, our dance team took part in the 'team rounds' and won — making us Division A champions! We left the ballroom at 11.30pm, happy and tired — but with enough energy for one more dance to celebrate our success!

FULL-ON GLAMOUR

Latin costumes are designed to dazzle, with sparkling sequins, jewels and tassles, coordinating colours and a body-hugging fit. But they must also let the dancers move their arms, legs and hips easily.

For the men

The man's outfit is modelled on a traditional suit: black dance trousers with a white or black shirt, or a stretch-fitted top. There may be a touch of glitzy decoration, fringing or flashes of colour to tie in with his partner's costume.

Type 'Latin dance competition' into www.youtube.com to see the competitors in full Latin glamour.

stunning samba headdresses add to the glamour of the carnival!

Accessorise

The most famous Latin dance accessories are the flamboyant headdresses worn by Brazilian samba dancers at carnival time. This glamorous headwear can include huge (feather) plumes, birds, fruit or flowers, and sparkling satin, beads or sequins – all in a riot of rainbow colours!

Longer legs

Women's dance shoes are usually heeled to lengthen the legs. This can make dancing difficult, so training sessions in heeled shoes are necessary to be able to dance comfortably!

spangled or sequinned dance shoes have ankle straps to help them stay on

Latin ladies

For women dancers, a glamorous, glittery or floaty dress is essential. A fitted, low-backed bodice helps the dancer move freely, while a swishy, flowing skirt flicks out with every wiggle of the hip. Crystals and beading are designed to shimmer and catch the light.

Fancy footwear

For men, dancing shoes with flexible leather soles slide smoothly across the floor without skidding, and allow the foot to 'feel' the floor.

dramatic make-up can help to create a dance 'character'

Fake it!

The audience and judges see dancers from a distance and usually under bright lights, so bold make-up helps to emphasise their features and adds to the drama of the dance. Women also often wear fake nails, eyelashes and fake tan to spice up their look.

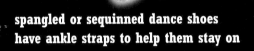

23

SUSANA MONTERO

Top Latin dance choreographer and winner of the UK Salsa Dance Championships, Susana has worked on star-studded shows such as *Strictly Come Dancing* and *So You Think You Can Dance?* Radar asks her the questions *you* want to know...

Why do you think Latin dance classes are so popular?

Latin dance has the feel-good factor! You can relax at a Latin dance class and really come out of your shell. Latin is such a social dance, too. It's a great excuse to forget your troubles and just have fun!

What is so thrilling about Latin dance?

Latin is the most passionate and emotional dance form. You feel an intense connection with your partner and this makes it such a beautiful dance to watch.

What's been your big career highlight so far?

Doing the choreography for *So You Think You Can Dance?* The competitors are so talented, professional and easy to work with. I hope watching this show inspires more people to express themselves through dance.

What is it like to work on the UK's *Strictly Come Dancing*?

Amazing! The atmosphere is electric and it's fantastic to watch the celebrities develop their skills and techniques. I love working on the show and contributing to the choreography – it's wonderful to see your very own ideas put into action!

How can Radar readers pursue a career in Latin dance?

It takes passion, determination and time. You have to be a perfectionist and practise every step over and over. If dancing is your passion, you'll have the drive to push yourself and improve your dancing to competition level.

Do you have to be good at other types of dancing?

Not at all – Latin is a great dance for beginners. As long as you love dance, you can Latin dance!

Did you start Latin dancing as a child?

No – from the age of five I had a passion for ballet and flamenco and learned both of these. I was introduced to salsa as an adult. The style of the dance totally gripped me and I haven't looked back!

Do you need a partner to start?

No partner needed! You can get started with salsa, samba and several other styles on your own, or in a group with everyone dancing solo.

25

THE PASO DOBLE

The paso doble is inspired by the drama and danger of a Spanish bullfight and is performed to a march-like beat. It is always danced in pairs: the male and female play different roles to bring this impressive dance to life!

The bullfighter

The male dancer takes the role of the bullfighter, or matador. Quick, dramatic movements show his pride and courage when he enters the ring. His chin is lowered as he watches the bull carefully. Strong arm lines, posture and powerful foot stamps show his confidence in the face of danger.

The swirling cape

The female dancer plays the role of the bullfighter's cape, spinning around the ring with long, sweeping steps. She may also act as the bull. Her robin tilts upwards to create elegant lines. Her dress is long and flows like a cape. Bold colours, such as black or deep red, add to the drama of the dance.

Strike a pose

Paso doble music features several breaks or 'crashes'. Routines are carefully choreographed to allow the dancers to strike dramatic poses at each break. The dance becomes more and more exciting as the battle between bull and bullfighter comes to an end.

Type 'paso doble' into www.youtube.com to see this dramatic Latin dance.

27

EASY RUMBA

The rumba is a super-slow dance also known as 'the dance of love'. The emphasis is on smooth, flowing body and hip movements rather than detailed footwork.

You will need:

- space to dance
- a dance partner
- rumba music

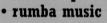

FEEL THE BEAT:
Angels by Robbie Williams

1

M Hold your partner's right hand away from her body, at shoulder height. Your right hand should be placed on her back. Step forwards onto your left foot, towards her right leg.

F Place your left hand on your partner's right shoulder. Step backwards onto your right foot.

2

M Step backwards with your right foot.

F Step forwards with your left foot.

3

M Slide your left leg to the side.

F Slide your right leg to the side.

M Slide your right leg in front of your left, bringing your body with you. Extend your right arm as your partner extends her left arm.

F Slide your left leg in front of your right, bringing your body with you. Extend your right arm out as your partner extends his left arm. This finishing pose is known as the 'New Yorker'.

4

Type 'rumba dance steps' into www.youtube.com to see the dance in action.

Got it?

You should have maintained the same hold throughout steps 1 to 3 before releasing the hold in step 4. Your movements should have been perfectly synchronised.

CARNIVAL!

It's the climax of the Rio Carnival. As your samba club's spectacular float waits near the sambadrome, you hear the roar of the crowd. Inside there are 100,000 people, all waiting to see you dance. Your body tingles with nervous energy and your mind races through the samba routines that you've practised all year through.

Sparkling sashay

Fireworks erupt like brilliant flowers of fire in the sky, signalling that it's time for your bateria to parade. Your heart beats faster. Every inch of your body sparkles with make-up, spangles and crystals. Huge colourful plumes sway above your head and cascade down to the floor. Despite the weight of your costume and the heat of the Brazilian night, you feel amazing.

The world is watching

Multi-coloured costumes gleam like rare jewels and headdresses shimmer and shake as you move in perfect timing with the passistas around you. It seems as though the whole country has stopped to watch the parade. Tonight, your sambadrome is the centre of the world.

Explosive energy

The atmosphere is electric as you dance at the world's biggest party. The driving pace of the surdo drums is so loud you can feel the beat in your bones. Huge decorated floats parade down the arena and hundreds of drummers bang out batucada rhythms, urging you to swing, shimmy and sashay to the beat of the music.

The party's hardly started!

You've been dancing for more than an hour, but it feels like five minutes. An adrenalin rush carries everyone out of the stadium to continue to party on the streets. The heat wraps around you like a blanket, but the carnival is just getting started. Party on!

LIVING LATIN!

Shimmy your way into one of the hottest dance scenes around by signing yourself up to a Latin dance class!

Search online to find classes local to you, or log on to websites:
www.dancesportcentral.co.uk or
www.danceschools-uk.co.uk

The BBC's *Strictly Come Dancing* website is another great place to find a Latin dance class near you – just type in your postcode to find your nearest class at:
www.bbc.co.uk/programmes/b006m8dq

Watch the pros

If you want to watch professional dancers compete, find lots of information about competitive events at:
www.dancesport.uk.com

DVDs & Apps

Check out Susana Montero's DVD lessons at:
www.monterouk.com

Download the *LDF Salsa Volume 1* app at:
www.iphonesalsa.com

Download the *DanceTimeLatin* app at:
www.wimbledonsound.com

INDEX